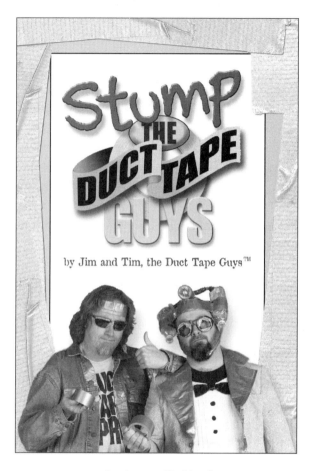

Stump THE DUCT TAPE GUYS

by Jim and Tim, the Duct Tape Guys™

**Andrews McMeel
Publishing**

Kansas City

05 06 07 08 09 BID 10 9 8 7 6 5 4 3 2 1

ISBN-13: 978-0-7407-5495-1
ISBN-10: 0-7407-5495-5

Library of Congress Control Number: 2005925089

ATTENTION: SCHOOLS AND BUSINESSES

Andrews McMeel books are available at quantity discounts with bulk purchase for educational, business, or sales promotional use. For information, please write to: Special Sales Department, Andrews McMeel Publishing, 4520 Main Street, Kansas City, Missouri 64111.

"If duct tape isn't the answer, then you must be asking the wrong question!"
— the Duct Tape Guys

Publisher's Note:

While many of the suggestions provided in this book are intended to inform readers about the myriad helpful uses of duct tape, others are intended only to entertain and should not actually be attempted by readers. Specifically, we caution you against applying duct tape or WD-40™ to any of the following: fish, dogs, cats, horses, any other animal, prospective employers, or Evelyn Wood. Our legal department would also like us to note that we are not responsible for injuries sustained to readers who tape themselves to moving vehicles. Thank you.

Duct Tape Guys Note:

Well, that pretty much voids the entire book.
So, you can either ignore the disclaimer
and proceed with reckless abandon or rip out
this warning page and give the book
to your worst enemy.

A Message
from the Duct Tape Guys:

For the better part of the past decade it has been our privilege to maintain the "Stump the Duct Tape Guys" portion of our Web site. Through this free public service we have provided counsel to those suffering everything from broken toasters to broken hearts. In the sampling that follows you will be exposed to the varied (and sometimes bizarre) problems that are plaguing your fellow citizens, and, like a good soap opera, it will make your life seem free and easy by comparison. You'll also pick up some great tips for utilizing duct tape to handle anything that life throws your way.

The Duct Tape Guys believe that duct tape can fix anything. In fact, the guys' motto since their first book, published in 1994, has been "It ain't broke, it just lacks duct tape." And that's the basic premise of this, their seventh duct tape book.

One of the most popular sections of their massive Web site (www.DuctTapeGuys.com) is "Stump the Duct Tape Guys," which invites readers to submit questions, problems, and situations that presumably cannot be fixed with duct tape. The Duct Tape Guys don their thinking caps (made entirely out of duct tape, of course) and come up with answers that have never failed to satisfy (if not amuse) their inquirers.

Here then, in no particular order, are a sampling of the questions posed by real people, and answered with wit and wisdom* by Jim and Tim, the Duct Tape Guys.

*Wisdom subject to change without notice.

My vintage 1976 self-winding watch no longer self-winds. How can duct tape fix my watch so that once again it will tell me the correct time more than twice a day?

We're thinking that a good smack to the watch would free the mechanism that makes it self-wind. In order to avoid damage to the crystal during the smacking operation, wrap your watch body in four to five layers of duct tape. Hold the watch by the band, and smack the watch on the face of a duct tape roll. If your watch doesn't work after this delicate procedure, rewrap the watch in duct tape and tape a little triangle on its edge on the top of the watch face, creating a wrist sundial that will never need winding—just a sunny day. —*DTG*

I'm a college guy who just can't seem to get a girl. Some of them call me ugly! How can duct tape help me look better and get a girl to go out with me?

Duct tape over your entire face and attend classes as "that mysterious duct tape mask guy." The intrigue will drive all of the girls absolutely nuts. You'll be able to get your pick of the pack. Keep your duct tape mask on through at least your first four or five dates. The girl will come to love you for the person you are inside, and not the way you look. —*DTG*

How can we use duct tape to get chewing gum out of my sister's hair without ripping her hair out?

Actually, we recommend WD-40 for getting gum out of hair. To avoid getting the gum into the hair next time, cover your sister's hair with duct tape. When you remove the tape your sister won't have any hair to worry about. Note: Your hearing will also be gone—due to the excessive screaming that duct tape stuck in hair creates. —*DTG*

Remember, besides duct tape, WD-40 is the only tool you need in your toolbox.

That's right, Jim. If it's not stuck and it's supposed to be, duct tape it. If it's stuck and it's not supposed to be, WD-40 it.

It's the yin and yang of your toolbox.

I drove my car into a telephone pole, and my license plate became embedded in the pole. How can duct tape get my license plate out of the pole and keep people from noticing the dent in the pole?

Duct tape the exposed edges of the license plate to your front bumper and put the car in reverse. The license should pop out of the pole. Now fill the dent in the pole with duct tape wads and tape around the damaged section of the pole. Duct tape is not a foreign element to most utility companies, so the repair should look quite natural. —*DTG*

Sounds like what happened
to your car, Jim.

Oh, ah . . . yeah it kind of does,
doesn't it? But it wasn't me that
sent that one in. . . . Hey, can I
borrow your roll of duct tape?

Sure. What are you going to
use it for?

Oh, nothing . . .

You're gonna go fix the phone pole
aren't you, Jim?

My sister recently gave me her old lava lamp. I plugged it in and waited four hours for it to warm up. I noticed that the lava stuff was making a bunch of small bubbles instead of the giant lava. How could duct tape solve my problem?

If you leave the lamp alone for a while and then plug it in again, the globs should be melded together. Replace the light bulb with a new one of recommended wattage (usually 40 watts); it should heat up more quickly.

Where does duct tape come into play? Duct tape yourself to a chair in the opposite corner of the room so you aren't tempted to monkey around with the lamp until it has time to acclimate to its new surroundings.

—DTG

My seventeen-month-old son is teething. How can duct tape help with the pain, but continue to let the teeth come in?

Make a big wallet-sized wad of duct tape for your kid to chew on. The teeth will be cut through in no time. —*DTG*

How can duct tape be used to trick the Breathalyzer when I get pulled over for drinking and driving?

We enjoy a good beer as much as the next guy, but drinking and driving? Even we aren't that stupid! We suggest that the police who pull you over utilize duct tape to bind and gag you while they're throwing you into detox. Then, when you sober up, they can duct tape you to the grieving parents of a teenager who has been killed by a drunk driver. This might help you think and drink more responsibly. —*DTG*

I play guitar, and when I strum my pick always hits the guitar and has worn a hole in the wood. How can duct tape repair this situation and not muffle the sound?

The sound shouldn't be muffled any more than if there were wood there. While you're at it, cover the whole guitar in tape and it will look like one of those steel guitars. —*DTG*

I'm worried that the government's proposed missile defense system is not going to be effective protection in the event of a nuclear exchange. How can we use duct tape to protect us from a nuclear assault?

Unfortunately, only roaches will survive a nuclear exchange. Therefore, we suggest that you wrap yourself entirely in duct tape, sticky-side out, and stick cockroaches all over yourself. No, you won't be very popular at work or school, but there's a better chance you'll survive a nuclear attack! —*DTG*

How can I travel back in time using duct tape?

We fail to see the desire to go back in time much past the 1940s, when duct tape was invented. Even if you could time-travel with duct tape, the tape would disappear prior to 1942 and there you'd be—stuck without duct tape. Travel back in time by reading history books. Use duct tape as a bookmark when you start getting drowsy. —*DTG*

How will duct tape keep rabbits and other pests out of my garden?

Duct tape laid sticky-side up around the perimeter of your garden will keep most varmints out while reflecting sun up onto the underside of your plants. —*DTG*

How can I use duct tape to remove ammonia from my pond water?

The ammonia is probably coming from the fish peeing in the water. Duct tape the fish so they don't leak and the ammonia will disappear. Or, better yet, save your money on fish food and other pond-cleaning supplies—grab a few rolls of colored duct tape and fashion your own exotic fish, like the one pictured here. —*DTG*

I'm trying to learn how to stop a
Slinky in midslink, but it's proving hard
to do. How can duct tape fix my problem
without mutating the Slinky?

Let's guess: You're getting a government grant for
this research, right? Put duct tape, sticky-side up,
on two consecutive steps. Start the Slinky down
the stairs. It will freeze when its two ends are
stuck on the two duct taped steps. —*DTG*

I enjoy listening to my old records from
the 1960s and '70s. Most of my older ones
are scratched up, the grooves are worn down,
and they don't sound as good as they used to.
Using only duct tape, how can I repair my old
records, making them sound as good as new?

Stuff duct tape balls in your ear canals and put a strip of duct tape over each ear. The muffled sound will hide all of the pops and scratches in your vinyl discs. —DTG

Hey, Tim. Do you know how many grooves the average LP record has on each side?

One groove on each side, Jim.

Oh, you heard that one before?

No. From start to finish, it would have to be just one groove per side; otherwise the needle wouldn't progress through the record tracks.

I never thought of that.

How can duct tape
stop my husband's snoring?

Make a duct tape ball and tape it to his back
prior to bedtime. The ball will make him roll to one
side or the other, reducing his tendency to snore.
Or you could put duct tape over your ears as
described in the previous hint. —*DTG*

My wife duct
taped a muffler
to my face.

Maybe she
should have put
another one on
your butt.

How can duct tape be used to sharpen an ax?

Duct tape the ax at the proper angle
to the rear bumper of your car or truck.
Drive around the block. When you get back home
you'll have a sharp ax! —*DTG*

Can you think of at least twenty things to do with duct tape, a chicken, and a garden hose?

Yes. —*DTG*

How can duct tape cure poison ivy?

If you duct tape your hands together
behind your back until the rash clears up,
you won't be tempted to scratch the welts, which
will control the spreading and speed the healing
process. Preventing poison ivy rash is where duct tape
works best. Before you go hiking, duct tape all exposed
flesh. When you return home, shower until all of the
poison ivy juices have been rinsed off the tape.
Remove and discard the tape. You will be rash-free
(unless you're allergic to duct tape glue). *—DTG*

**I don't have very good eyesight and it's hard
for me to read the small type on my computer
monitor. Can duct tape help this situation?**

Most computers have a way to enlarge the font size. Or you could purchase one of those big magnifying sheets that people put in the rear window of their motor homes and tape it over your monitor. Better yet, use duct tape to repair everything you might be tempted to pay a high-priced professional to fix. Take all the money that you have saved and use it to purchase a larger monitor. —*DTG*

Tim, I don't have a computer. How can duct tape help get my e-mail for me?

It can't.

Ha! I stumped you!

You're ineligible, Jim!

I think you mean incorrigible, Tim.

Suppose I'm an astronaut alone in a space station. Suddenly, a meteorite knocks a hole in the wall and everything starts getting sucked out into space. I'm able to grab a roll of duct tape floating by. How could the duct tape save me?

It depends on how extensive the damage to the space station is. If the tape on the roll will contain the damage, tape quickly and you're set. If not, at least you'll die happy with that roll of duct tape in your hands. —DTG

If I were rock climbing and fell, assuming I had a roll of duct tape handy, how could I use the duct tape to save myself before plummeting to my death?

While falling, quickly remove your shirt and fasten a long strip of duct tape folded over onto itself to each of the four corners of your shirt. Use this shirt as a parachute to float yourself safely to the ground. —*DTG*

I have been trying to learn how to play guitar for quite some time now, and I just can't seem to get it. How can duct tape speed up my progress?

Tune the guitar to an "open chord." Wrap duct tape around the index and middle fingers of your left hand and use them as a slide. Presto! You're playing guitar! —*DTG*

I play tuba in my school band, and our tubas are _really_ dented and ugly. Since our budget doesn't allow for new tubas, how can duct tape help us not look stupid when our marching band plays at our upcoming football games?

First, fill the dents with little wads of duct tape. Then tape the entire instrument with white duct tape—it will look like one of those fancy white, fiberglass tubas. Or send school spirit soaring by taping over each tuba in one of your school colors. —*DTG*

Hey, tape guys, what makes the sticky stuff sticky (on a molecular level)? Is there anything it won't stick to and, if so, why (again, on a molecular level)?

Haven't you heard that you aren't supposed to sweat the small stuff? All you have to know is that it sticks. Why ask why? As for what it won't stick to: Duct tape doesn't stick on wet stuff. So if you are going to make yourself a duct tape swimsuit, make sure you aren't all sweaty from thinking about small stuff, or you'll find yourself doing some inadvertent skinny-dipping. —DTG

That's not what you told me, Tim! There I was, totally naked in the pool with my duct tape swim trunks hanging from the diving board!

You just weren't listening, Jim. I'm pretty sure I told you to dry off first.

Stump THE DUCT TAPE GUYS

I live in an old house. How can duct tape help me conserve energy this winter?

Most likely, your windows aren't as tight as they used to be. Tape around the wooden sashes to prevent leaks. Duct tape clear plastic sheeting over the outside of each window to further prevent drafts. You may also feel cold sneaking in through electrical outlets on exterior walls. A small strip of tape over each unused outlet will seal these leaks as well. (First make sure your duct tape doesn't have any metal in it; most duct tape doesn't.) —*DTG*

How can duct tape be used to take the faces off Mount Rushmore and restore it to its natural mountain face?

Perhaps you didn't know it, but those faces were actually inside the face of the mountain all along and were revealed only after painstaking removal of the zillion tons of rock that were obscuring them. And what a remarkable coincidence that they resembled four of our presidents! I guess if you wanted to cover them back up, you could just duct tape the removed rocks back into place. —*DTG*

Here's an interesting note: On the back side of Mount Rushmore, there are four big stone butts back there.

Oh yeah? Why don't they show that in the travel brochures, Jim?

It's too embarrassing.

My grandpa loved duct tape. Unfortunately, he passed on. Can duct tape bring him back to life?

If your grandpa loved duct tape, just thinking about all of the ways he used duct tape will keep his memories alive for you. Every time you grab a roll of duct tape or spot duct tape quietly doing its job somewhere, it will be like your grandpa is looking down at you and smiling. As long as you have your memories of your grandpa, he's right there with you. —*DTG*

I am lost in the labyrinth of the Minotaur. I fear he may find and attack me at any moment. There is a roof covering the top of the labyrinth so I can't climb out. The only items I have with me are a couple of rolls of duct tape. How can I get out of this maze safely?

For your sake, we hope this is a hypothetical question. First, make a replica of yourself out of duct tape and stand it in plain view. Then wrap yourself in duct tape, sticky-side out, and hide in a corner and wait for the Minotaur to pass in your direction. As he attacks your duct tape replica, fling yourself against his hindquarters—the sticky-side out tape will adhere you to the beast. Then, undetected, you can ride him to safety (most Minotaurs eventually leave the labyrinth in search of water). —*DTG*

Those labyrinths are *amazing* aren't they, Tim? "maze," get it? Labyrinth . . . maze.

Yeah, I got it. Good one, Jim.

How can duct tape keep the algae from growing in my pond?

You can use duct tape to stop algae from growing in a pond. Just cover the pond with an opaque tarp made from duct tape. Since algae need sunlight to grow, the darkness provided by the duct tape cover will prevent the growth of algae. —*DTG*

I work with a bunch of Mexicans. Sometimes I get mad at them because they like to speak in their language so that nobody else can understand what they're saying. How can duct tape help with this problem?

Duct tape a Spanish dictionary to your arm.
Soon you'll learn enough Spanish to understand
what they are saying and even join in their
conversations. You'll also figure out that
Mexicans are normal people just like you
(we're assuming here that you are normal).
Unencumbered by fears of people unlike yourself,
you'll broaden your little world, develop new
friendships, and have a richer life to boot. —DTG

Is there a way that duct tape can make old paintings (like the Sistine Chapel ceiling) look as vibrant as the day they were painted?

Art restoration experts carefully remove the crud covering up old paintings. I suppose that duct tape, if used very carefully, could accomplish this task with great success. Speaking of the Sistine Chapel ceiling, did you know that a portion of the ceiling shows God handing a roll of duct tape to Adam? —*DTG*

I have attention deficit disorder. Can duct tape help me?

I'm sorry—we weren't paying attention.
What was the question? Nah, just kidding. . . .
Duct tape yourself to whatever you are
supposed to be paying attention to. —*DTG*

If I were out in the woods with just a roll of duct tape, how could I make a hot shower?

Make a big duct tape hammocklike bag suspended between two trees to collect rainwater. When the rain quits, seal the top of the bag to prevent evaporation. The sun will eventually heat the water in the bag. When the desired temperature has been reached, stand under the bag and poke a small hole in the bottom of it to dispense the heated water. When the bag is empty, put a strip of tape over the hole, reopen the top of the bag, and wait for more rain. Or just find a local campground. They usually have shower facilities. You can trade your roll of duct tape to the grounds attendant for a hot shower. —*DTG*

Hey, Tim. If you were in the forest and ripped a strip of duct tape off the roll, and a tree fell with nobody around to hear the tape rip off the roll, could you fix the fallen tree with duct tape?

Don't you have something you're supposed to be doing, Jim?

Could duct tape have stopped the technology sector of the stock market from falling?

If America relied more on duct tape and less on technology the stock market would be more stable. Consider the word "crashed," as in "my computer crashed" and "the stock market crashed." Coincidence? We don't think so. Invest in duct tape and you'll never be disappointed. —*DTG*

I work full-time and I own a dog. I'm never home to walk him, but I love him to death, so I won't give him away. Is there any way duct tape can help take my dog for walks?

We believe it was Sting who once said, "If you love someone, set them free." If you really loved your dog, you would either give him away or get home earlier so you could take him for walks. Why not use duct tape at your place of employment to shorten the time it takes to accomplish your job? You will be able to leave earlier and get in some canine walking time. —DTG

Can duct tape help extend the range and accuracy of my paintball gun?

Duct tape a longer barrel on the gun. Spray the inside of the barrel with WD-40 to prevent friction when the paintball exits the barrel. As far as accuracy, duct tape a tripod to the bottom of the gun to help steady your aim. —*DTG*

How do I use duct tape to start a fire?

Duct tape a stick to your leg and run around in circles until the stick bursts into flames because of friction. (Caution: This hint may result in a burning sensation on your foot and/or leg.) You might also want to duct tape an airsickness bag to your face to avoid the mess and embarrassment when you get dizzy from twirling around for up to fifteen minutes. —*DTG*

My car windshield leaks water and I tried duct taping over the edges. It worked fine for about a month, but due to high air resistance from driving, it peeled off. I also live in Minnesota, so cold temperatures would have a negative impact on its adhesion. Can duct tape still help me?

Spare the tape and spoil the job! You're either using a substandard tape or not enough of it. We recommend a UV-coated duct tape to prevent the tape from delaminating due to exposure to the elements. To increase adhesion in the cold, warm the tape with a hair dryer during application. —*DTG*

How can world hunger be solved using only duct tape?

Tape over the mouths of the affluent in the world after they have reached their daily requirements of food. Then share the wealth of resources that are not consumed with those less fortunate. —*DTG*

How can duct tape help me win the Boston Marathon?

Booby-trap the marathon course by placing duct tape, sticky-side up, on the starting line. Make sure you spray the bottoms of your shoes with WD-40 so you don't stick to the tape. Or just duct tape yourself to the nearest Kenyan. —*DTG*

I thought of another way you could win the marathon, Tim. Just duct tape yourself onto the lead camera vehicle.

Good idea, Jim.

Thanks, Tim.

How can I exercise using duct tape?

Place multiple large duct tape rolls on both ends of a broomstick for a makeshift barbell. Or pull off a strip of duct tape about three feet long, double it over onto itself, and make a loop at both ends. Use this as a resistance pull for isometric exercises. —*DTG*

I am in the military, and the patent leather shoes I wear are constantly getting scuffed. Once scuffed, they are useless. How can duct tape stop the scuffs without ruining the military spit-polished appearance?

Black duct tape is really shiny—just like your military-issue shoes are supposed to look. Cover them in this tape and you'll have a nice shine and prevent scuffing at the same time. —*DTG*

Hey, look, Tim. I can actually see my reflection in my shoes.

Are those mirrors duct taped to your shoes, Jim?

Yeah. Hey, look, there's gum stuck under the table.

**How can I get flowers
(plastic or otherwise) to stick to
tombstones? They keep falling off!**

Wrap the stone with duct tape,
all the way around. Tape the flowers
to the duct tape and they won't fall off. —*DTG*

I broke a taillight on my car and repaired it with duct tape, but the light didn't show through the tape. Is there a better way to make this repair?

You can correct major damage with duct tape. As for the transparent red plastic over the lamp, you must resort to lesser tapes. They have a special clear red tape for this very purpose available at your local auto supply store. Make sure you secure this lesser tape with more duct tape around the edges. *—DTG*

I work in a restaurant where we serve a great cheeseburger. How can duct tape make our burgers the talk of the town?

Jim and I are suckers for a good cheeseburger. All you have to do is provide us with an endless supply of your burgers and we'll provide you with our Duct Tape Guys endorsement. That should help propel your sales through the roof. Or you could serve your cheeseburger on a duct taped paper plate. —*DTG*

I'm addicted to duct tape. I'm duct taping everything! Is that a known fetish?

No, that is absolutely
normal and healthy behavior. —*DTG*

As I run around the shop, barking orders and giving directions to my employees, my coffee cup doesn't seem to be able to keep up with me! I spend valuable time looking for my lost coffee cup. How can duct tape fix this problem?

Duct tape your coffee cup into your hand. Or skip the cup and duct tape damp coffee grounds to your arm to make a caffeine patch. —*DTG*

**I have a cat that has a scratching post
but instead prefers to use the couch.
What can I do?**

Put duct tape, sticky-side out, on the place you want
the cat to stay away from. The cat will scratch it once,
get stuck to the tape, and never scratch it again,
whether the tape is present or not. —*DTG*

**I have a hundred-pound rottweiler with a bad
attitude and a bad case of fleas. The vet won't
touch her. How can duct tape help with the
flea problem?**

Encase your entire dog in duct tape.
No more fleas, no more shedding, and, eventually,
no more dog! —*DTG*

Stump the Duct Tape Guys

My office PC keeps crashing. Our company's computer nerds can't seem to fix it. Can duct tape help?

Wrap your PC in duct tape and use it as a boat anchor or doorstop. Then go out and buy a Macintosh. —*DTG*

I'm going on a cruise but I can't swim. Are there any precautionary measures I should take?

Yes, we suggest duct taping unopened potato chip bags onto your arms. That way, if you fall overboard you can stay afloat until you learn how to tread water. Then you can open the bags and have a supply of food until you're rescued. —*DTG*

I lost a library book somewhere in my messy house. How can duct tape help me find it again?

Do what we do: Cover yourself in duct tape, sticky-side out, and roll around the house gathering up all the loose objects. Have your roommate pick the stuff off you and either put it where it belongs, file it, or throw it away. Continue rolling until the book shows up. (It is customary to give your assistant any money that is found during this process.) —*DTG*

I like to customize my clothing with duct tape, but the duct tape falls off in the washer and I don't want to keep replacing the duct tape every time I wash the clothes. What should I do?

No problem! Make your clothing entirely out of duct tape and you'll never need to wash it. Just hose yourself off once in a while. —*DTG*

Is it possible to make a
sharkproof suit out of only duct tape?

If you use enough duct tape (about eighty layers),
the shark shouldn't be able to bite through it.
However, you would probably still be squished to
death in a shark attack, leaving your crushed body
firmly preserved in the duct tape suit—like a
massive metallic mummy. Then again, even if you
survived the jaws of the shark, you would probably
die a claustrophobic death from being wrapped in so
much duct tape. If you want to dabble with dangerous
fish, better stick with baby piranha. Just cover your
finger in about eight layers of tape and plunge
your finger into the tank. —DTG

I accidentally drove my SUV through the
back wall of my garage, down a twenty-foot
drop, and into a flowing stream full of raw
sewage. The tow company says there's
nothing they can do except let the car sit.
Is there any way that duct tape
could help me salvage my SUV?

No duct tape needed here.
Count your blessings and go out and find a more
fuel-efficient car. —*DTG*

I just got a new bike and don't care to have it stolen (like my last one). Is there any way that duct tape can prevent bike theft?

To avoid the heartache of a stolen bike, simply cover the entire frame with duct tape into which you have woven barbed wire (available at your local farm/ranch supply store). Would-be thieves will think twice before touching your bike. Just make sure you are extra careful and sit bowlegged when you ride the thing, or you will be using duct tape as a bandaging material for your own cuts. —*DTG*

My prostate is the size of a grapefruit. How can duct tape help me fix this?

A couple of strips of duct tape, strategically placed, will prevent you from wetting your pants while you make your way to the phone to schedule surgery. —*DTG*

My moose is on fire! What do I do?

Obviously, you weren't cut out for moose ownership, since only neglect could have caused this situation. Too late now. Go out, buy some buns, and then settle back and enjoy some mooseburgers. Use duct tape to remove any remaining moose hair from the burgers before you eat them. —*DTG*

If I were blinded and fell into a lake, how would duct tape help me get ashore?

Only a rigorous training program will help you should this situation arise. To do this, simulate blindness by covering your eyes with duct tape. Walk backward into a lake, then walk back to shore. Do this many times, going farther out each time. Eventually, you will be able to handle blind swimming with no problem. In fact, for you lap swimmers with chlorine-sensitive eyes, cover your eyes with duct tape to prevent the redness. Just feel for the lane ropes to maintain your course. —DTG

Stump the Duct Tape Guys

I take really bad pictures. How can duct tape help me become a better photographer?

Duct tape the camera to your face, allowing one eye to see only what is in the viewfinder of the camera. Soon you'll be recognizing the difference between a real photo opportunity and stuff that is just commonplace. When you see a great frame, just reach up to the camera and click the button. —*DTG*

I'm really tired of emptying the dishwasher. How can duct tape relieve me of this chore without creating any new ones?

Tape the dishwasher door shut. This will prevent you from loading it, and thereby you'll never have to unload it. Then duct tape over paper plates to create some strong, disposable plates. —*DTG*

I can never seem to get my Kool-Aid to taste right. It's always too sugary or not sweet enough. How can duct tape help?

Duct tape the Kool-Aid package instructions to the side of the appropriately sized sugar-measuring cup. —*DTG*

Stump the Duct Tape Guys

My sister plays the organ and tends to
slip off the front of the wooden organ bench.
She won't let me put duct tape sticky-side up
on the bench because she doesn't want the
sticky goo on her dress. How can I help her?

Make her a special organ-recital dress out of
duct tape. Build in two little squares of duct
tape, sticky-side out, on the "butt" area of
the duct tape dress. This will stop the sliding.
It may also gain her notoriety as the
"Duct Tape Organ Diva" and
boost her career. —*DTG*

**I went to a horse show and my horse
pulled up lame. Is there anything
I can do to fix his foot with duct tape
so I can jump him in the next class?**

Duct tape is always a staple in a tack shed
and at the large animal vet. Just tape the horse's
leg up real good; this will give it the extra strength
it needs to heal up quickly. —*DTG*

**My little kitten keeps coughing up
hairballs. Is there any hope for her
with the use of duct tape?**

Sure. Just feed your cat little balls of sticky-side out
duct tape. As they move through the cat's system, the
fur will stick to the duct tape balls and pass right
through to the litter box. —*DTG*

The choke on my 1983 AMC Eagle refuses to work when it's colder than thirty-five degrees outside. Is there any way to fix this situation with duct tape?

Duct tape a heating pad to the engine's temperature sensor and it won't know that it is less than thirty-five degrees out. In the absence of a heating pad, you can substitute a little kitten. (Just kidding.) —*DTG*

My computer screen is fuzzy. Can duct tape fix it?

Yes. Purchase some reading glasses. Punch out the lenses, and duct tape the lenses right over your eyes. The screen will sharpen right up. If it doesn't, you might want to duct tape your head into a paint shaker and turn it on for about three minutes. Then everything will be fuzzy, making the computer monitor look normal. —*DTG*

Which came first: the chicken, the egg, or duct tape?

Duct tape wasn't invented until the 1940s—
so we'll take a wild guess and say that the egg
came first, followed by the chicken, and then
duct tape (which comes in handy when
constraining your chickens so they
don't cross the road). —*DTG*

I recently lost my two front teeth while playing soccer. It's very hard for me to chew my food and talk. How can duct tape help me?

Make some duct tape dentures. You can use
either white duct tape, silver, or yellow
(for the vintage British look). —*DTG*

I'm trying to get a new job. Can duct tape convince my prospective employer to hire me?

Yes. Bind and gag them with duct tape and only release them when you're hired and they've signed a nice severance package for you. —*DTG*

I've wanted to start snowboarding but I don't have money for the equipment, so I was wondering if I could make a snowboard out of duct tape?

Make a supersized snowboard by duct taping your boots to an upside-down ironing board and hitting the slopes. —*DTG*

STUMP THE DUCT TAPE GUYS

I'm a vegan and wanted to know if there are any types of animal products in the tape's adhesive?

Have you ever heard of 100% Pure Pork Duct Tape? Neither have we. No, duct tape is made from a rubber-based adhesive, plastic, and a cloth mesh (from plant or synthetic sources). And, by the way, it's *not* edible. So, as much as you might be tempted to eat it as a meat substitute, we wouldn't recommend it. —*DTG*

I'm a drummer. Is there any way for duct tape to keep me from throwing my sticks?

Just drink eight cups of coffee before your next gig, tape your sticks to your hands, lower the sticks toward the drum heads, and you'll be doing one-handed rolls to rival Buddy Rich, no problem! —*DTG*

How could duct tape have prevented the fall of the Roman Empire?

Heck, if the Roman Empire had had duct tape, it would never have fallen. Rome would have been the dominant world power to this day! Unfortunately, duct tape wasn't invented until World War II, when the U.S. military needed a way to keep the moisture out of ammunition cases. Now look who's the dominant world power! —*DTG*

Stump THE DUCT TAPE GUYS

My favorite NFL football team is in third place in their division. How can duct tape help them win?

Duct tape the hands of your receivers, sticky-side out. Then duct tape the yard lines sticky-side up and don't tell the opposing teams. Talk about home-field advantage! —*DTG*

My hollandaise sauce has separated. How can I repair this with duct tape?

We'd suggest putting the hollandaise in a jar and duct taping the jar to a jackhammer. The vibration will remix the sauce in no time. Remember to share your sauce and your duct tape with the workman who lent you his jackhammer. —*DTG*

The light on the on-off button on my cordless phone is bothersome at night. How can I turn it off with duct tape?

Duh! Just duct tape over the light. By the way, this also works on the flashing "12:00" on your VCR. —*DTG*

I've been playing the cello for four years, and I would like to think that I am pretty good. Some of my songs require really hard bowing, which is tough on the horsehair on my bow. How can I keep the bow hair from breaking on me?

We've never tried it, but we imagine that duct tape around your bow, sticky-side out, would make a really fine, durable alternative to the bow hair. And since duct tape is made from synthetic material, there would be no bald horses as a result of your cello playing. —DTG

I am seriously into dance. In dance, flexibility means everything. My splits to the front are pretty good, but my side splits are somewhat lacking. How can I use duct tape to improve my flexibility when doing side splits?

Stand with each foot duct taped to a chair. Have a friend slowly move the chairs apart. You will gain flexibility that you never knew you were capable of as your butt plummets toward the floor.
By the way, duct tape and a couple of paint-stirring sticks make great splints for broken ankles. —*DTG*

Here in New England, we get a lot of leaves in the fall. I'm tired of raking those suckers. How can duct tape help me?

Invite the neighborhood kids to your yard for a game of football. Before the game, duct tape their feet and legs, sticky-side out. By the time the game is over, your leaves will be gone. —*DTG*

I live in Pittsburgh and my office is in Singapore. I fly twenty-seven hours each way once a month to go to work. How can duct tape make this unbearably long flight shorter?

Call a taxi. Duct tape a note to your chest that says, "Take me to the airport and load me on flight #3." Make sure you have your boarding pass and enough money for the cab fare attached to the note. Then duct tape a bunch of bricks precariously over the front door of your house. When you open the door as you leave for the airport, the bricks will fall on your head, rendering you unconscious. The taxi driver will read the note, load you in the cab, take you to the airport, and get you on the flight. You should regain consciousness somewhere near your destination. For the duration of the flight, duct tape ice to your head to ease the swelling and the resulting headache. It's that simple! Happy travels! —DTG

**How do you fix a computer
after dropping it off the Sears Tower
in Chicago with the broken components?**

We can only imagine that you are running a Windows
machine. Switch to a Macintosh and you won't be so
tempted to throw your computer off the Sears Tower.
Most duct tape users are of a more practical, simple,
grassroots ilk, and therefore they make great
Macintosh users. By the way, duct tape can also
help you construct your sentences in a more
grammatically correct, logical order. Cut up your
sentence and rearrange the words until they
read better. Then stick the newly reorganized
sentence onto duct tape. —*DTG*

Who is Red Green and what is he famous for? And who exactly came up with duct tape first—you guys or Red Green?

Red Green is another duct tape evangelist (and Ontario TV show host) from the Toronto area. He uses a ton of duct tape in his show and calls it "the handyman's secret weapon." Neither of us "came up with duct tape" first—that was the U.S. military during World War II. However, we both recognized and capitalized on the humor potential of duct tape at about the same time. Garrison Keillor also created the fictitious sponsor "The American Duct Tape Council" for his *Prairie Home Companion* around that time. None of us were aware of the others' efforts. There must have been an aligning of the duct tape planets or something that gave rise to this collective duct tape consciousness. —*DTG*

I'm in an electronics class in school, and I have a slight problem. Due to a shortage in school funding, we ran out of the wire needed to complete our circuits. How can duct tape help, since it doesn't conduct electricity?

You might want to do what other schools have done to raise funds. Sell strips of duct tape for a dollar a strip and let the students use it to tape the principal to the wall. You'll probably raise enough funds to buy the wire you need for your little electrical project. —*DTG*

Stump the DUCT TAPE GUYS

I have a gas fireplace in my house and it won't work because the gas is not coming out. What should I do?

Your gas isn't coming out because you probably forgot to pay your gas bill. Here's a great way to remember your bills: Use duct tape to make a giant month-long calendar grid on a wall of your house. Next, duct tape your bills in the grid four or five business days before each bill is due. Each day, check the calendar for bills you have to mail that day. You'll never miss a payment again! —*DTG*

I can play the trumpet, but I can't play very well. How can duct tape help me improve my trumpet playing?

Dizzy Gillespie was a great trumpet player, and he had those really big, puffed-out cheeks when he played. We suggest that you make two two-inch-diameter duct tape balls and stuff them in your cheeks. You will probably become instantly better on the trumpet, or at least look like you are really trying hard. —*DTG*

The coating on my nonstick frying pan is peeling off. Can duct tape help?

We've heard that it's not good to use those pans once the coating starts to separate. Duct tape over the top of the pan as a reminder to throw the pan out and get a new one. Or recycle! Make a burglar alarm out of the old pan. Next time you leave for vacation, hang the pan over your entry door by one strip of duct tape. Rest the business end of the pan on top of a piece of cardboard that you have duct taped to the top edge of the door. When the door is opened, the pan will fall on the head of the intruder (or on you, if you forget that you put it there). —*DTG*

Stump THE DUCT TAPE GUYS

How can we use duct tape to stop my obsession with the TV show *Friends* while still allowing me to enjoy other programs?

Duct tape over the *Friends* channel button on your remote control. As an added measure of safety, duct tape over the TV listings so you can't find out when it's broadcast. Better yet, get some real friends for yourself by starting a duct tape enthusiasts group. You'll no longer feel the need to waste your time watching fictitious friends. —*DTG*

How can I make a weather station using only duct tape?

Attach one end of a strip of duct tape, folded over onto itself, to a tree branch. That's it! That's all you need. Use the chart below to interpret and report the weather after consulting the strip of duct tape. —*DTG*

If the duct tape is:

Cool to the touch—it's cold out
Warm to the touch—it's hot
Wet—it's raining
Dry—it's not raining
Still—it's calm
Moving—it's breezy
Horizontal to the ground—it's windy
Missing —there's a tornado

Stump THE DUCT TAPE GUYS

Several years ago, I attempted to cover
a window in my cellar with a clear sheet of
plastic. I tried to tape the plastic to the cellar
wall, which is painted concrete. In a few
weeks, the duct tape failed and began to pull
away from the wall. Is there any way I can
get the duct tape to stick to the wall?

The problem is that cellar walls are usually
either moist or dusty. Duct tape will not stick to
moist or dusty surfaces. We suggest that you first
waterproof your cellar and wipe the surfaces clean.
Then rent a gas forced-air heater and run it in
combination with a dehumidifier until the walls
are bone dry. Now you can tape the plastic over the
window with ease. Remember, spare the duct tape,
spoil the job. Use plenty of tape! —*DTG*

What is the best way
to get duct tape off clothing?

Pull off the duct tape. Then spray any remaining
residue with WD-40. Let it sit for a while, then wash.
Repeat as needed until both the adhesive and the
WD-40 residues have vanished. —*DTG*

My hair gel keeps leaving a sticky film on my palms. How can duct tape help me with this problem?

Tape over your hands before applying the gel. Remove the tape from your hands after you are done styling your hair and they will be gel-free. Or forget the gel and just duct tape over your entire cranium! You'll be sporting the most popular hairstyle around! Your hairdo will never need washing and certainly won't be mussed by the wind. —*DTG*

I suffer from dry, red eyes when driving. How can duct tape help me with this without impairing my vision?

Heating and air-conditioning vents blowing at your face are probably causing the dry-eye problem. We recommend making duct tape baffles over the vents to divert the airflow toward your feet. Unless you are very short, this should take care of the dry-eye problem. —*DTG*

How can duct tape help me get over a chest cold?

Try duct taping several mustard packets to your chest to create a "mustard plaster" just like Grandma used to recommend in the treatment of a cold. I used this method and, by golly, if the cold didn't totally disappear in just three weeks! —*DTG*

I was working in my lab and i accedentaly spliced the wrong jean. Can ductape fix it?

Juging frum yer speling, you aint no scintist! So we can only assume that you mean mending your blue jeans. Do what we do: Duct tape your hems up, and reinforce the "wear spots," like the knees, pockets, and butt areas. Your jeans will last years longer, resist tears, and if you spill on yourself while barbecuing, you can just hose yourself off. —*DTG*

Can you use duct tape to demonstrate in a sensible manner why we have eyebrows?

Just stick a strip of duct tape, sticky-side out, over each eyebrow. At the end of the day, you will be able to examine all of the junk stuck to the tape and therefore prove that your eyebrows are very effective in keeping all that junk from going into your eyes. However, they'd be even more effective if they were as sticky as duct tape! —*DTG*

I am planning on proposing to my girlfriend next week. How can duct tape help me?

Do what Jim did to get his wife: Duct tape yourself to her leg and don't remove yourself until she accepts your proposal of marriage. —*DTG*

Your pants are way too small and won't fit.

How did you know our pants were way too small?
Do what we did: Just cut out the back seam of your
pants, splitting it down to the bottom of your butt.
Then spread the split seam and use duct tape to
create a V, expanding the waistband up to ten inches.
Your pant legs can easily be lengthened by adding
strips of duct tape around each cuff. This also
prevents heel wear on the pant cuff. —*DTG*

Can duct tape fix a major crack in the transmission on my truck? It leaks about three pints a week.

If you wrap anything with enough duct tape it will stop leaking. However, we suggest that you do what we did (our truck leaks about two quarts a week). Duct tape a funnel under the transmission where it is leaking, duct tape a hose onto the funnel, and route the hose up into the filler tube that goes to the transmission. Halfway up the hose route, duct tape a small wind-driven pump that will activate as the vehicle goes down the road. This will pump the dripping transmission fluid from the bottom of the vehicle and route it right back into the transmission. This works with oil pan leaks, too. Just route the hose into the oil filler cap and not the transmission. —*DTG*

I have an old tractor that leaks gas at the valve near the knob you turn to switch the gas on and off at the bottom of the gas tank. Can duct tape fix that?

Since gasoline dissolves the glue on duct tape, we suggest that you duct tape a large funnel underneath the drip, duct tape a hose to the funnel, and run the hose back into the gas tank (yeah, just like the transmission fluid hint above). —*DTG*

How can our freshman orchestra members use duct tape to give our orchestra seniors a nice good-bye tribute?

The first thing that comes to mind is a complementary duct taping of all of their instrument cases. We've yet to see an instrument case that hasn't been (or couldn't be) enhanced, repaired, and strengthened with duct tape. —*DTG*

I am not allowed to use sharp implements
of any kind after cutting up the wife's credit
cards. She says anything that can inflict
that much pain on her should be locked up.
Thanksgiving is just around the corner,
and now I am stuck with the problem of
slicing the turkey. How am I going to
accomplish this with duct tape?

Duh! You should have just duct taped over that
magnetic strip on her card, rendering it useless. No,
wait . . . then she would have taken away your duct
tape! No sir. You did the right thing. Not only that, you
got out of the horrendous duty of carving the turkey!
Good thinking, man! We laud your creativity! You are
an inspiration to men everywhere! —DTG

Someone just gave me a fish tank. It is a
hexagonal tank, so you can see through it,
but it has a crack in one of the sides.
How do I fix the crack so that I won't be
able to see the crack or any other
blemishes on the tank?

Repair the crack with clear duct tape. Then duct tape
a mural onto the cracked-glass side of the aquarium.
We suggest the great pyramids or some other desert
scene. This will make the fish glad that they are where
it is cool and wet rather than hot and dry. Or you can
just cover all of the sides with duct tape and pretend
that there are fish swimming inside. This will save
you a bundle on fish food and prevent you from
having to ever clean the tank. —*DTG*

I'm a senior in high school and am attempting the impossible task of choosing where— or even whether—to go to college. Can duct tape end this misery once and for all?

Duct tape is a staple at most colleges we have visited, so wherever you choose to go, you will find a common bond with duct tape. I suggest covering your ceiling with duct tape, sticky-side down, and throwing all of your college catalogs up into the air. Most of the catalogs will stick to the tape but then eventually fall again, one by one. The last one remaining on the duct tape is the college you should attend. This will probably be the lightest catalog, usually meaning fewer classes and more party time.

Tape on, dude! —*DTG*

My friend ran into a deer on his way home one night, and it bent his radiator to the point that it kept the engine from running well. We would have tried to turn the radiator around so the bent faced out, but it won't fit in the body molding that he already bought. Is there anything that can be done without having to replace the radiator or without duct taping the radiator outside the body molding?

We think your thought of duct taping the radiator to the outside of the vehicle is a great idea! Go with that one. In fact, you have motivated us to make the same vehicular enhancement to our truck—which usually runs a bit hot. By the way, to prevent other run-ins with deer, duct tape one of their natural predators to your hood (like a hunter). —*DTG*

Stump the Duct Tape Guys

I want to get into this band, but they will only let me play if I bring my own homemade electric guitar and can play it like Jimi Hendrix. To complicate matters, the only instrument I have ever played is the triangle.

Forget them. Start your own all-duct tape band: You are the leader on the triangle (dangling from a duct tape strap, of course). Other players must create their instruments out of at least 30 percent duct tape. This will not only create a unique "New Age" sound but will also provide you with a novel marketing angle that will be sure to attract the media. It shouldn't be too long before you'll be featured on the cover of *Rolling Stone!* —DTG

How can I use duct tape to prevent my refrigerator from falling through the floor of my trailer house?

Duct tape turns any appliance into an under-the-counter appliance. In the case of your refrigerator, you may want to use about a case of duct tape to secure it in position. —*DTG*

Which is more authentic: the Canarsie or the Weehawken style of mambo?

We have absolutely no idea what you are talking about. Therefore, we cannot possibly be stumped by your question. —*DTG*

I'm an aircraft mechanic. When I sign off my repairs in the aircraft logbook, those pesky FAA inspectors keep asking for the Maintenance Manual references to each repair. How do I get around this requirement?

Duct tape the Maintenance Manual to the logbook and tell them that you have attached all of the references. —*DTG*

Would duct taping big *X*'s over the prices on local gas-station signs help lower the cost of gasoline?

Here's a clever idea. Wrap duct tape around the end of a long pole, sticky-side out. Now reach up and use the sticky tape to remove the first "2" from the $2.25 per gallon on the station's sign. Suddenly, $2.25 per gallon becomes $ .25 per gallon. Fill up your tank and then pay only $ .25 per gallon "as advertised." —*DTG*

I have trouble bending over. How can I use duct tape to help get my shoes on?

Do what we do: Tie your shoes loosely, then duct tape over the laces. This will turn any pair of shoes into slip-ons. Put a doubled-over strip of duct tape right into the heel of each shoe. This will act as a built-in shoehorn. Now you should be able to easily step into your shoes without bending over. Or if you don't need to change pants often, just duct tape your shoes onto your pant cuffs. —*DTG*

I have a cat that was born unable to hear or see. How can duct tape restore my cat's sight and hearing?

Duct tape hearing aids can be made for your cat by forming large megaphone-type cones that you secure to the cat's ears using more duct tape. As for the ability to see, unless you can make rods and cones that are small enough to be implanted into the cat's eyes, you will have to settle for creating an enhanced "Whisker Alert System" for your cat. Extend and sensitize the cat's whiskers by applying duct tape strips to their ends. You can also fashion a large duct tape "bumper" in front of kitty's head to prevent her from getting injured when she does run into stuff. —*DTG*

I just turned fifteen and will soon be taking my driver's test. Can duct tape help me remember everything I learned in driver's education and help me pass the test?

Absolutely! Create what we call a "Knowledge Magnet" by duct taping around your forehead, sticky-side out. This will help the information that your instructor throws at you "stick" and soak into your head through a process similar to osmosis. During your driving test, duct tape your hands to the wheel at the 10:00 and 2:00 positions. Good luck! —*DTG*

Is there a way to learn Spanish using duct tape?

Yes! Bring a case of duct tape to Mexico and trade it for private tutoring! They should give you at least a month of room and board and private lessons for your kind gift. —*DTG*

Why was duct tape called "one-hundred-mile-per-hour tape"?

The army calls it that because it is used to hold stuff onto target drones that travel at speeds of up to one hundred miles per hour. That's one story—ask three others who were in the army, and you will probably get three more. —*DTG*

We use duct tape on our old pickup truck, Tim.

Yeah, so?

We should start calling it
thirty-seven-miles-per-hour tape.

Catchy, Jim.

How do we remove the adhesive left on the carpet from the duct tape?

That's why they have "gaffers' tape"—to hold stuff to floors and carpets without leaving a residue. But, apparently, it's too late for that now. The adhesive can be loosened with either WD-40, Goo Gone, or a similar product. Let it soak in for a while to liquify the adhesive. Then follow with a foaming carpet cleaner. After a while, the goo should vanish.

It's worked for us. —*DTG*

Stump the DUCT TAPE GUYS

I have to construct a DNA model of eighteen inches in height with a different section symbolizing the A, G, T, C, sugars, phosphates, and hydrogen bonds. And it must hold the pattern (for the left side) **GATTACACCA** at least once and twist twice. How can I do this with just one roll of duct tape?

We have no idea what you are mumbling about, but making a DNA model should be easy. Just make little duct tape balls and hook them together with rolled duct tape "sticks." Who knows? You may have just stumbled upon a stronger DNA model! —*DTG*

As you know, seat belts are required by California law. Mine fell apart, so I made new ones out of duct tape. A policeman noticed it and gave me a ticket. How can duct tape get my ticket excused so I don't have to pay the fine or have the violation on my record?

Take it to court and do a side-by-side comparison of your duct tape seat belts against the original, factory-installed belts in your car. If your car is old enough, it should become apparent that the duct tape belts are stronger than the aged fabric belts. You, therefore, are even safer than with a conventional belt. Just make sure your belt is composed of at least four layers of duct tape and it should be no contest! —*DTG*

**My room began to stink.
So I thought I would get creative and
duct tape a spring-scented dryer sheet to
my fan. To my surprise, duct tape doesn't
stick to dryer sheets! Any ideas?**

All you have to do is make a duct tape ring
on the face of the fan and stick the dryer sheet
through it. Either that, or clean your room! —*DTG*

How can duct tape help me prove that the universe is expanding?

Duct tape will not stretch (much), so put a
six-inch strip of duct tape on the street outside
your house. Then measure exactly six inches on the
pavement beside the strip and denote the six-inch
mark by driving a nail into the pavement. In a couple
of years, check the tape. If it is shorter than the
marked-off six-inch measure, you'll have proof
positive that the universe is expanding
(or that duct tape shrinks). —*DTG*

Let's say my house is on fire and I
make it out, but my baby is inside. By this
time, all the entrances and windows are
surrounded by fire. And there are no
neighbors home, so I can't call the
firefighters. How can I use
duct tape to save my baby?

If this is not a hypothetical problem, we'd prefer
that you not waste your time typing a note to some
Duct Tape Bozos! If this is a hypothetical problem,
we'd like you to take this opportunity to get
some yellow or red duct tape and mark a fire-
evacuation route on the walls of your house
so you are prepared if and when
a fire does happen. —DTG

Stump THE DUCT TAPE GUYS

If you are lost in the Sahara Desert with only your shoelaces and a trusty roll of duct tape, how can you survive off the duct tape for seven months?

Why seven months? Will you be rescued in seven months? How do you know this? Why only shoelaces? What happened to your shoes and the rest of your clothing? Why only one roll of duct tape? What kind of fool are you, and how did you get into this ridiculous situation? Answer these questions first, and we will oblige you with an answer. —*DTG*

I play the violin, and it has a large crack on the front. How could I use duct tape to fix the crack without compromising the quality of the sound?

We play a ukulele in our Duct Tape Guys' stage show. On our first trip, the airlines did a number on the instrument by dropping the suitcase the uke was in. The body of the uke cracked into three pieces. Well, it wasn't broken, it just lacked duct tape. We taped the body back together. Now it not only sounds better— more of a mellow tone—but it also looks like one of those expensive steel guitars (only smaller). So repair boldly and proudly with duct tape. Let the tape show. Like a teddy bear that gets worn, it is a step toward your violin becoming "real." —*DTG*

> Jim, tell them about your other uke modification.
>
> Oh, yeah. The neck broke off, so I reattached it to the body with a duct tape "hinge." Now it's a folding travel ukulele.

How can duct tape fix the hole in the ozone layer?

Send up a few cases of blue duct tape on the next space shuttle and have them tape a giant patch over the hole. Since there is no gravity up that far, the patch should just float in place as an ever-present reminder to watch our pollution and take care of our planet. —*DTG*

**My dad remarried and I now live
with my mom. How can duct tape improve
my relationship with my stepmother?**

Our plan involves evangelizing your stepmother on
the gospel of duct tape. Once you have shared the
many uses of duct tape with her and presented
her with her very own roll (in her favorite color),
you two will have something in common. Issue the
challenge of coming up with four new uses for
duct tape each time you get together. It will give
you something to talk about, and she will start
looking forward to your visits. —*DTG*

**My wife and I are trying to potty-train
our two-and-a-half-year-old daughter, but
she isn't cooperating. We tried duct taping
her to the toilet, but it left a rash and
the sitter called Children's Services.
How else might duct tape help us?**

You're approaching the situation wrong. Don't duct
tape your daughter to the toilet seat! Use duct tape
as the reward for going "big-girl potty"! Just have a
roll of duct tape and a little chart in the bathroom
next to her potty chair. Whenever she makes the
effort to go potty, give her a little square of duct
tape to put on the chart. If her effort is productive,
give her two squares! She'll be potty-trained
in no time! —DTG

My sister and I fight over the computer all the time. How could duct tape help us share?

Duct tape a clock to the top of your computer monitor. Put a little piece of red duct tape on the number 12 and a piece of green duct tape at the number 6. When the big hand hits the red tape, your sister has to stop and relinquish the computer to you. When the big hand reaches the green tape, you have to stop and give your sister a turn. Assuming that either of you aren't color-blind, this should work fine. —*DTG*

**My wisdom teeth are coming in.
Can duct tape help me get them out
without paying for an oral surgeon?**

Buy a ticket to the drag racetrack. Dry off the
tooth (so the duct tape sticks) and attach one
end of a twelve-foot strip of duct tape to the tooth
and the other end to the back of a drag-racing
vehicle. When the light hits green, your tooth
(and quite possibly the whole side of your face)
will be removed. —*DTG*

What kind of musical instruments can you make out of duct tape?

If you duct tape the open end of a pan, barrel, or oatmeal container, you've got yourself a drum. If you duct tape a funnel to a hose, you've got yourself a horn. Duct tape a broomstick to an upside-down washtub, fold a length of duct tape into thirds, and attach one end to the top of the broom handle and the other to the middle of the washtub. Presto! You've got yourself a "gutbucket." —*DTG*

You know, Tim. I think duct tape itself should be considered a musical instrument. Pulling it off the roll makes a really cool sound. And the faster you pull, the higher the pitch.

Good point, Jim. Why don't you go and compose a duct tape symphony?

**I recently had a bad breakup
with my girlfriend. How is duct tape
going to fix my broken heart?**

Breakups are often caused by "duct tape envy"—
a situation in which one partner doesn't share the
duct tape with the other. I know it sounds
impossible, but many men feel that duct tape is
specifically a "guy thing" and tend to hoard the
duct tape, or keep it hidden in that special drawer
in their workbench. Well, come on, guys! Duct tape
is gender neutral! Share the tape! Or, better yet,
give your mate her own roll. We're sorry about
your breakup and suggest that you go out and
get a roll of duct tape for yourself and one
for your ex. Maybe this gift will patch things
up and get you on the right road
to a long relationship. —DTG

**UV radiation can damage skin and eyes.
I wonder how this problem
can be fixed with duct tape?**

We suggest that you cover all of your exposed skin
with duct tape (any color will do). It's 100 percent
UV protection on a roll. And wear a pair of those
"old-people sunglasses" (you know, the oversized
sunglasses that are made to fit over eyeglasses)
and duct tape their lenses down to little slits
like those German vehicle headlights during
World War II. This will minimize your
exposure to the UV radiation. —*DTG*

We were out studying the tide pools in my marine biology class when the tide came in and covered the area before we could finish looking at stuff. How could we have used duct tape to fix this situation?

What we'd suggest is that you build a huge dam wall (we're not swearing) by placing four-by-eight sheets of plywood duct taped together around the exploration site. This should give you a few more hours of exploration. If the water gets too high, you can use the dam walls to float to safety. —*DTG*

I have tried to get my ten-year-old sister to stop talking! I tried a good name brand of duct tape to bind her hands and to cover her mouth, but she always escapes. What should I do?

Well, it's obvious that:
1) You don't like your sister, 2) Your sister's talking is bothering you, and 3) Your sister is Houdini reincarnate. So: 1) Find something that you and your sister have in common (like duct tape), 2) Talk about the virtues of duct tape so her talking isn't so bothersome to you, and 3) Profit from your sister's escape talents—sell her to a carnival sideshow. —*DTG*

I tried to fix my wrecked radio-controlled airplane with duct tape, but the duct tape doesn't seem to stick to it. What should I do?

Clearly, you are either using an inferior brand of duct tape (there are cheap impostors out there), or the plane is wet (duct tape does not stick to anything wet), or you are not using enough duct tape (spare the duct tape, spoil the job). So figure out which is your situation and try again. If at first you don't succeed, tape, tape again. —DTG

You wrote that one, didn't you Jim?

Why?

Where's my airplane, Jim?

I don't know what you're talking about.

How can I alleviate those monthly female cramps?

We're not female, but we can imagine that female cramps are the closest thing a female experiences to getting kicked in the privates. To prevent that from happening, we've duct taped a plastic salad bowl to the crotch of our pants. It's kind of a commedia dell'arte look (you know that Italian comic theater stuff). So try the duct taped salad bowl idea and let us know if it works for you. —DTG

I built a snow fort outside that must have
been at least seven feet tall. But now
it's starting to melt and get holes in it.
What should I do?

Obviously, you missed Snow Fort Building 101,
where they teach the "cheat method" of getting large
appliance boxes and covering them entirely in
white duct tape, thus avoiding the need
for snow altogether. —*DTG*

We've said it before, and we'll say it again—spare the duct tape, spoil the job. Just supertape the bowl—it will look like a fine pewter serving service. As for the melting: Make sure the tape you are using is certified as *duct* tape. To legally be labeled *duct* tape, it has to meet certain heat-resistance standards (as it is often used on ductwork). Our thinking is that you have been duped into using some cheapo, noncertified duct tape impostor. —*DTG*

I broke a piece of DRAM in half. How can I fix it?

Jim once had a ram that kept butting him with his horns. He duct taped a pillow over the horns and cut down considerably on the bruising of his posterior. Since the "*D*" in DRAM probably stands for "duct," we see no reason why you can't just tape the two halves together and go about your business. —*DTG*

I currently have the flu. How can duct tape help?

We're no medical experts, but when we have the flu, we use duct tape over both ends and go to work as usual. —*DTG*

Sorry about your legs. We have no idea what a Rotorblade is, but we imagine that it's probably been outlawed in most states. Here's your fix: Get out your duct tape, grab a couple of two-by-fours, and duct tape them to your leg stumps. Duct tape a pair of shoes to the bottom of the boards. You will be able to walk around at normal height again. If you wish, you could even add a foot or two to your height just to impress your girlfriend. She'll soon be proud to be seen with "that real tall guy." Who knows, make yourself tall enough and you might also get a contract with the NBA! —*DTG*

Stump THE DUCT TAPE GUYS

My sink keeps dripping, and it keeps me awake at night. Without totally sealing off the faucet with duct tape, how can I remedy the situation?

Take a strip of duct tape, connect it to the faucet head, and let the length of the tape dangle onto the sink-basin floor. The water will quietly trickle down the duct tape and into the drain without making that annoying dripping noise.

Sleep tight! —*DTG*

My boyfriend's mustache tickles me when we kiss.

Duct tape over the mustache and give it a good rip!
It's like bikini wax on a roll. Or, if he likes to have
a mustache, go for a big, black Groucho Marx
greasepaint mustache made out of black duct tape.
It certainly worked to make Groucho a ladies' man.
And unlike greasepaint, it won't get your face
all black when you kiss him. —DTG

My dog is continually scratching our wood floor while racing to the sliding glass door to bark at squirrels. How can I prevent this?

Make little duct tape slippers for your dog so his claws don't scratch the floor. Either that, or just duct tape entirely over your wood floor and remove the tape only after your dog has moved on. —*DTG*

I have brown hair. Everyone says blondes have more fun, but no dye I've ever used seems to work. Can duct tape make me a blonde?

Two ideas come to mind. Cover all exposed parts of your body (except for your hair) with duct tape and allow the sun to bleach the heck out of it. Or skip the sun altogether and use yellow duct tape (or white if you prefer platinum blond) to create a duct tape hairdo in any style you choose. This is our preferred method. We are both members of the Duct Tape Hair Club for Men. Duct tape hair never needs washing—just a dusting or hosing off every two to three weeks. Have fun as a blonde! —*DTG*

My favorite tree just got struck by lightning, and it split in half and fell. Using duct tape, how can I put the tree back together and have it still look the same as it did before it fell?

Consider this a godsend! Move a portion of the tree into your house and decorate the branches with leaves made from colored duct tape. You can change the color with the season or keep them green all year long. Then sit back and enjoy your favorite tree in the climate-controlled comfort of your own living room! —*DTG*

**I was drinking my favorite drink
(Jolt Cola—which is hard to find where
I live), but before I could finish the can,
it went flat. Is there any way that
duct tape could have helped?**

Next time, put a little tab of duct tape over the
hole of the can when you're not drinking and it will
retain the carbonation longer. —*DTG*

I'm in science class, and I just threw a beaker of sulfuric acid at the door and made a big hole in it. If I try to put duct tape on it, the duct tape will just melt. What should I do?

Quick! Sit in a chair and wrap duct tape around your feet. Then put a strip over your mouth and eyes. Finally, put your hands behind the chair and wrap the tape around your wrists. When the teacher returns to the classroom and finds you, explain that some vandals overpowered you while you were doing your lab assignment. This should get you off the hook for the damage to the room. Have your teacher clean up the acid mess— they're trained to do that. —DTG

I was wondering if it's possible to get double-sided duct tape and, if so, would I be able to use it to give my car a waterproof seal?

Double-sided duct tape? Just roll it over into itself, sticky-side out, and you have double-sided tape! Or just seal your car doors shut with duct tape and crawl through the windows like Bo and Luke Duke. —*DTG*

We are tired of letting our dog out to go to the bathroom. How can duct tape help us?

Duct tape a kitty litter box to your dog's hind end. She will be so humiliated walking around with the litter box attached to her that she'll learn to use the porcelain fixtures. —*DTG*

My computer is way too slow.
How can duct tape speed it up?

Duct tape your computer to a greyhound. —*DTG*

How can duct tape
ease the pain of childbirth?

Just have your childbirth coach hold a roll of
duct tape in front of your face. Concentrate on
the tape and its powers. This has worked for us
when having bullets removed (don't ask) without
any anesthesia whatsoever. Another option is to
put a duct tape "headband" wrap around your
head and make it so tight that the pain of the
duct tape headband distracts you from any
pain in your southern regions. —*DTG*

I have braces and they really hurt my cheeks. How can I fix my problem?

All you have to do is dry off your teeth (and braces) and put a couple of layers of duct tape over your teeth (like a sports mouth guard). This will prevent the wires from going into your cheek. Use white tape and you won't even look like you have braces on. —*DTG*

I have a bike and plenty of duct tape. How can I go to Mars?

Simple! Just duct tape yourself and your bike to the next rocket going to Mars. —*DTG*

I am short. Is there any way duct tape can make me taller?

Sure. Duct tape bricks onto the bottoms of your shoes—you will be at least three inches taller immediately. Then hang from the rafters of your garage with the bricks duct taped to your shoes and you will eventually stretch your legs for permanent height gain. Good luck! —*DTG*

I've got another idea for how duct tape can make you feel taller, Tim.

What's that, Jim?

Duct tape boards to all of your door frames, lowering the top of the door opening by about two feet. You'll be hitting your head on the door frame just like a basketball pro.

**I got this migraine that you can't believe!
My head feels like it's in a vise!
Can duct tape help me?**

As a fellow migraine sufferer, I've actually used
duct tape to alleviate the symptoms of my
migraines. Duct taping an ice pack or can of cold
pop behind your neck will often help. Since my
migraines are food related, I duct tape my mouth
shut whenever I am tempted to eat "trigger foods."
If it's too late for that, and the migraine is making
you nauseous, duct tape an airsickness bag to
your face and go about your duties. —*DTG*

It is now legal to collect, cook, and eat roadkill in North Carolina. How can duct tape assist with this newfound food source?

Cool! Attach strips of duct tape to your back bumper. Let the strips dangle onto the roadway. Start your vehicle and drive. You're trollin' for roadkill! —*DTG*

I lost my wallet last week, and I can't find it anywhere. How can duct tape help me find it?

Attach strips of duct tape to your back bumper. Let the strips dangle onto the roadway. Start your vehicle and drive. You're trollin' for lost wallets! After you find it, do what millions do: Throw your wallet away and duct tape your money to your thigh. Cut a hole in your pants pocket so you can reach in and retrieve your cash when you need it. —*DTG*

I'm a guitar player and I broke my G string. What should I do?

Sorry, this book is G-rated. We don't talk about nude guitar players' needs. (Off the record, we think the answer is rather obvious. Use the duct tape for the G . . . ahem . . . string.) —*DTG*

How can I entertain myself through a three-hour school play with just a roll of duct tape and a can of WD-40?

What more do you need? Sneak around the theater and duct tape the ripped upholstery in the theater seats and spray the seat pivots with WD-40 so they don't squeak. —*DTG*

I have about a week to get two F's up to at least C's, or I can't go to California with my friends in two weeks. How can I use duct tape to solve this problem?

Take a strip of duct tape and rip it to the width of the lines of the F in the grade book. Put one short strip coming out at a right angle from the bottom of the F and another strip going vertically from the bottom of the previous strip to the top line of the top right of the F. Repeat on the other F. There, now you have two B's. Have fun in California! —*DTG*

My neighbor's dog has telepathic powers. The dog keeps on barking in my head! The dog is keeping me up all night! Please help me!

Since the barking is only in your head, you must *think* about duct taping the dog's mouth shut. This will solve the problem. —*DTG*

Stump THE DUCT TAPE GUYS

I want to get my math homework done, but I don't have time. Can I use duct tape to solve the following question? If $(4x + 1)(x - 2) = (2x - 3)(2x + 3)$, what is the value of x?

Cover a sheet of paper with duct tape and hand it in. When the teacher asks you where the answer is, tell them it is under the duct tape. When they remove the tape, it will destroy the paper, thus obscuring the fact that you didn't really have the answer. When your teacher asks you to perform the solution again, tell them that you think it's unfair, since they destroyed your work. Get the principal and the school board involved. You'll probably earn an A for your creative problem-solving ability. —*DTG*

I am a theater technician and I need to hang a seventy-five-pound lighting instrument from an electric grid two hundred feet in the air and I have no ladder, hoist, crane, or boom. How can duct tape get the fixture two hundred feet above the deck?

Find a tech assistant who weighs seventy-six pounds. Attach a duct tape harness around the tech's armpits and above their head. Fold a four-hundred-foot-long strip of duct tape over onto itself three times. Attach one end to a three-pound rock and one end to the seventy-five-pound light, around which you have wound duct tape sticky-side out. Get your star quarterback to throw the rock over the lighting grid. The rock will come back to the theater floor with the trifolded duct tape attached to it. Remove the rock and attach the assistant to the trifolded duct tape. Get a weight lifter to hoist the assistant up to the grid. When the seventy-six-pound assistant is on the grid, have them cut off exactly one half of the trifolded duct tape (leaving two hundred feet). Then have them jump off the grid with a grid rung between them and the seventy-five-pound light. When the assistant goes down, the light will go up. The light, surrounded with the sticky-side out duct tape, will stick to the grid when it arrives. Reattach the three-pound rock to the now two-hundred-foot trifolded duct tape and have your star quarterback toss it up into another section of the grid to get it out of the way.

It's that simple! —*DTG*

I had to duct tape two stages together. I did. I created a fuse that was solidly duct tape. It was one inch thick. The initial strokes were long ones connecting the two bars of the legs of the stage. Then, these were strengthened with strokes going between the bars and fusing the starting strokes. This was continued, alternating between the long binding strokes and the strengthening strokes in between (which strengthened and also prevented any moisture from getting to the core) until it was one inch in diameter and solid. Now, this binding was undone after the show by the work of two Leatherman saws. My question is, how would you undo it using only duct tape and WD-40? Remember, it was crosshatched so that liquids (such as WD-40) can't get inside.

Wow! You lost us after "I had to duct tape two stages together." We have absolutely no idea what you are talking about, or what the problem is. Lock yourself in a room with a roll of duct tape and a can of WD-40. We're sure the answer will come to you. —*DTG*

I love toast, but my toaster just broke. How can I fix it?

Throw that ugly appliance away. Buy one of those heat lamps that restaurants use to keep your food warm while your server is out back having a smoke. Make a duct tape hammock under the lights. Lay the slices of bread on it, where they can relax and bask in the warm glow until they sport a golden tan. —*DTG*

I have horrible asthma, and I often can't breathe. Without covering my mouth with duct tape, how can you fix my problem?

Assuming that your asthma is affected by dust, pollen, and other allergens, I suggest that you make a filtering breathing apparatus to filter those substances out. Here's how you make it: Get a cardboard toilet-paper tube and line it with duct tape sticky-side out and as many folded-over, sticky-side out strips of duct tape as you can fit in lengthwise while still allowing air to pass through. Duct tape this contraption to your mouth and duct tape your nostrils shut. The stickiness of the duct tape will capture the dust, pollen, and other allergens as you inhale (and also trap your bad breath as you exhale). In other words, you can breathe easy with duct tape! If you want to take deeper breaths, use a paper-towel tube. —*DTG*

My VCR keeps "eating" tapes. How can I fix this situation?

The reason that your VCR ate your tape is that it was gummy from the film that gathers on the head (or capstan). This is a problem that will cause us to grab the only other tool in our toolbox. Spray WD-40 on the components and wipe them clean with a cotton swab. Removing the WD-40 residue is important, because while it will loosen the dirt nicely, it will not disappear on its own accord and will eventually grab more dust and get gummy. Now that the dirt and grime particles have been loosened, your machine shouldn't have any more appetite for tapes. If this doesn't work, we suggest that you duct tape the door to your VCR shut so you are not able to insert any more tapes. —*DTG*

My mom says I can only stay on the Internet for thirty minutes a day. How can I prolong my surfing time without getting in trouble with my parents?

Show your mom educational sites like www.DuctTapeGuys.com and she'll no doubt become convinced that the Internet is indeed a valid educational tool. She may go so far as to not let you eat dinner until you've spent three or four hours doing your "research" on the Web. —*DTG*

This is one problem that is worldwide and can't be fixed with duct tape: PMS!

Don't be so certain. Let's look at the symptoms of PMS: bloating and irritability. To take care of the bloating issue, just duct tape yourself up tight enough to prevent bloating and water retention. As for the irritability, find something to repair with duct tape. It will keep your mind off what is irritating you and provide you with a sense of accomplishment that will fill your spirit with happiness that will last you at least ten minutes. Repeat as necessary. —*DTG*

Recently, while playing hockey, I got hit in the foot with a puck. The metal skate blade broke. How can duct tape repair the skate?

Knock the blade off your other skate and duct tape two pizza cutters to the bottom of each boot. There! You've got yourself some "Italian Rollerblades." They'll work on ice, too! —*DTG*

My cat and dog were joined at the hip after a nasty experiment in the laboratory. How can duct tape fix this situation?

I think your cat and dog will probably fix themselves. But keep your duct tape handy— you'll probably be using it as a bandaging material. —*DTG*

How do you avoid burnt lasagna using duct tape?

No problem—we burn our baked pasta dishes all the time. All you have to do is get a piece of duct tape and write the phone number of your local Italian restaurant on it. Tape it near your telephone. Next time you get the craving for lasagna, pick up the phone, dial the number on the duct tape, and make reservations! —*DTG*

There's this guy I really like. How can duct tape and WD-40 make me more attractive to him?

Enhance your chances of being liked by any guy by spraying a bit of WD-40 on your pulse points, and show liberal use of duct tape on your apparel. Any guy who can resist the smell of WD-40 or the sight of duct tape isn't worth having. —*DTG*

My house is burning down! How can I use duct tape to stop the raging fire?

Obviously, by the time we got your letter, your house was already a pile of ashes. Next time dial 911 instead of taking time to write for advice. To prevent this from happening again, cover all your walls, doors, windows, and cracks with duct tape. This way, there will be no oxygen in the house, and without oxygen, a fire will not burn. —*DTG*

Problem: My cat is stupid.
How can duct tape fix that?

There is probably nothing wrong with your cat.
As far as we've been able to tell, all cats are stupid.
Either that, or they're actually extremely smart
and just act like complete, brainless zombies so that
nothing will be expected of them (which, come to
think of it, is a pretty good idea). To elevate your
cat's intelligence, duct tape it to the ceiling. While
your cat is figuring out how to get off the ceiling,
go out and buy yourself a dog. —*DTG*.

You really don't like cats do you, Tim?

I didn't say that, Jim. I think cats serve a very important purpose in some people's lives. For me, they serve the very important purposes of making me sneeze, causing my eyes to puff up, and adding a nice layer of fur to my pants whenever I sit on your couch.

See, they're not all that bad!

I have a trampoline in the backyard
of my home. It is so old and used that holes
are appearing in the tightly wound fabric.
Single-strip patches never stayed in place, so
I covered the entire trampoline with strips
of duct tape. It works great! But all of
my neighbors think I am a freak.
What should I do?

We doubt that your neighbors' thinking that you're
a freak has anything to do with your trampoline
or your use of duct tape. You might consider
shaving and getting a job. Either that, or do
what we do: Ignore them. —*DTG*

I live in Hawaii, and volcanoes can be a hazard. If Kilauea Volcano is spewing hot lava and a gargantuan flow is rapidly heading for my house, can duct tape save my house?

Use the duct tape to construct a large hot-air balloon. Secure the balloon to the roof of your house. Unbolt your house from its foundation. As the hot lava approaches your house, the hot air will fill the balloon and lift your house above the dangerous lava flow. —*DTG*

My cat is grotesquely obese. She eats all the time. We tried to put her on a diet, but she snuck snacks on the side. What can we do?

Bind your cat entirely in duct tape except for her head and "bathroom apparatus" and let her eat. Her swelling body will become so uncomfortable in the unyielding duct tape corset that she will eventually cut back on her eating. —*DTG*

Note: Hints in this book that suggest applying duct tape to cats (or other domesticated animals) are not endorsed by the ASPCA or any other animal-rights organization.

There, that should serve as an adequate disclaimer, right, Jim?

What? I wasn't listening.

Never mind.

I've got a hot date this weekend and want to impress her. How can I use duct tape to my advantage but not let it steal my spotlight?

Duct tape the entire inside of your car. Make silvery vinyl seats, silver dashboard, woven silver headliner, duct tape roll can holders on the dash . . . take it to the limit. If your "duct tape limo" handiwork doesn't persuade her that you are a quality, caring guy, dump her and find a gal who appreciates duct tape as much as you do. Compatibility in relationships is paramount to lifelong happiness. —*DTG*

How can I use duct tape to help me win concert tickets on our local radio station?

This is an easy one! Any rock-and-roll roadie worth his salt is a huge fan of duct tape. So bring a whole case of duct tape to bribe the roadies. It'll probably even get you backstage passes. Works for Jim and me every time! —*DTG*

I got sucked into a parallel universe where everything, including duct tape and WD-40, works in reverse. What should I do?

Just use your duct tape to loosen things and your WD-40 to hold stuff together. We assume that aging in that universe works in reverse, too. So eventually you will need to remember to use your WD-40 to reseal your disposable diapers. —*DTG*

We have triplets. How can duct tape reduce our huge disposable-diaper bill?

If you check the diapers and they're not soiled, use duct tape to reseal the tabs. You might also do what Jim's parents did. Using those disposable diapers that say "Good for eight to ten pounds," they duct taped around the waistband and leg holes and fit twenty to thirty pounds in them . . . —*DTG*

I am studying very hard right now for my French finals. Can duct tape help me?

Duct tape slices of French toast, some French fries, French roast coffee beans, and a French dip sandwich to your head to get yourself in the proper frame of mind for the test. But seriously ... duct tape means never having to say *"Je parle français."* Drop your stupid French class and study the language of duct tape—it's universal! —*DTG*

I'm a telemarketer. When someone says they want to be taken off a call list, it means it's against the law to call them again. I forgot to mark down one of these requests and was fined five hundred dollars. How can I use duct tape to avoid being assessed this fine again?

Just duct tape your phone headset to the floor and stomp on it until it's no longer functioning. That way you won't be getting the fines, you won't be bothering us during dinner with your ridiculous offers, and you'll probably get fired, to boot—thereby freeing yourself to find a more fulfilling job. —*DTG*

Stump the DUCT TAPE GUYS

Your on a flight to a "Duct Tape Convention" when your plane, which just happens to be a small six passanger sesna type commuter .... goes down on a desserted island. You and your six passangers are lucky to have made it out of the reckage ... as you look at the badly recked plane (as everyone turns to you to fix it) you realize you are almost out of duct tape! You have a 1"x 8" peace left! Now none of the others have duct tape either, and your spare duct tape was burned in the reckage. (Being of a highly flamible nature as you know!) But the plane hasn't been burned totally you think it looks salvigeable. So now how do you use your piece of duct tape to help get you out of this situation?

There are some problems with your question:

1. Duct tape is not highly flammable.
2. A Duct Tape Guy would never find himself in a situation with a limited supply of duct tape.
3. Duct Tape Guys do not travel in Cessna-type planes.
4. There are no duct tape conventions (yet).

Not to mention your abundance of spelling and grammatical atrocities in your hypothetical situation. So, no answer for you! Back to the drawing board you go! —*DTG*

My mother absolutely loves the smell of lilacs. However, she cannot keep them alive for long. Can duct tape keep the lilacs alive longer?

Wean your mother from the smell of the lilacs by blending it with the wonderful smell of just-ripped duct tape. Wrap the vase holding her lilacs with duct tape—it will look like a lovely pewter vessel and provide added protection if she happens to drop it. Your mother's brain will gradually replace the true lilac smell with the hybrid duct tape–lilac smell. By the time the lilacs die, she will still have the duct tape smell. Just add a few new strips every month to keep that pungently refreshing duct tape smell alive.

You could also craft some everlasting lilacs using green and purple duct tape. —*DTG*

Stump the Duct Tape Guys

My friend was behind my snowmobile riding on a car hood that I was towing. We rounded a corner and *bam!!* He hit a parked hay baler. We were moving at approximately fifty-five to sixty miles per hour. Is there any way that duct tape or WD-40 could have prevented such a horrific scene?

Well, duct tape and WD-40 can't prevent you from being stupid (it still hasn't helped us). Our thought is to take two car hoods and sandwich your friend (wrapped in Bubble Wrap) between them. Duct tape around the hoods, spray them down with WD-40, and go for it! When he does happen to hit something, you'll most likely need the Jaws of Life to remove him from the metal sandwich, but he will probably still be in one piece. —*DTG*

The post office seems to keep mangling the letters I send to my girlfriend. How can I create indestructible stationery using duct tape?

Write or type your letter as usual, then back the entire sheet with two layers of crisscrossed duct tape strips. Trim the sides neatly and place the letter in a large duct taped envelope. If the post office does happen to mangle this, the goo on the tape should gum up their handling machines to such an extent that they'll exercise more caution in the future. —*DTG*

Got any stamps to mail this letter, Jim?

I don't use stamps, Tim. I just duct tape my letter to the back of a bus driving to where I am sending the letter; then I call the recipient of the letter and tell them to meet the bus at the bus station to retrieve their letter.

The long-distance call probably cost you more than a stamp would have.

Oh. I hadn't thought of that.

My car key broke off in the door lock. How can I get into my car?

You can duct tape around your fist and smash out the side window (the duct tape will provide protection from the broken glass). Or use a rock to smash the window. To make sure you are always prepared if you find yourself in this situation, duct tape a rock in a wheel well of your car. —*DTG*

There is a time bomb in my kitchen with a note that reads, "If tampered with, this bomb will destroy the entire planet." How do I prevent the destruction of the planet?

Well, for heaven's sake, don't mess
with the thing! —*DTG*

I am working on an oil painting for my art class. It is due to be hung in an art show tomorrow and I just ran out of yellow paint. I really need it and it is too late to go to the store. All I have is a roll of duct tape. What can I do?

Hopefully it's a roll of yellow duct tape. If not, use the tape (presumably silver) in the spots where the yellow is to appear, then wear a bright yellow jumpsuit to the opening of your show. Make sure you stand directly in front of the painting all evening. The duct tape will reflect your outfit, appearing yellow. The painting will no doubt command a higher price and sell more quickly due to your implementation of the duct tape. —*DTG*

**My skateboard busted into a million pieces.
I don't have money for a new one.
What can I do?**

You should have taped over the board when it was brand-new to prevent this from happening. Too late for that now. . . . So, fashion a new board with about fifty layers of duct tape woven together into the shape and size of the board you dream of! Tape on the wheels and do that grind thing you do on a new silvery, extra-durable duct tape board! —*DTG*

How can duct tape get me out of a speeding ticket?

Cover your car entirely in black duct tape so it looks like a stealth fighter. This should make it virtually invisible to radar. If you should get pulled over, you can claim to be a special agent with the Department of Homeland Security and say that you are testing the new government-issued stealth vehicle. Tell the officer, "Apparently, there are still some problems with the cloaking device. Thanks for letting me know. Give me your badge number and I will be sure that you are sent a commendation." —*DTG*

Without getting into trouble with the child welfare department, how can I keep my kids quiet using duct tape?

Nothing keeps preschool, elementary, even college-aged kids busy and quiet like a roll of duct tape. They can create sculptures, decorate their apparel into hip duct tape fashions, and even make up games using duct tape. So give them a roll or two and tell them to be creative with it. Remember, duct tape comes with no instructions (which is a good thing, because it doesn't limit your creativity). At first, they may look at you like you're nuts. But after they experience the power of duct tape, they'll thank you for it. —*DTG*

**How can I make my spaghetti sauce
tastier with duct tape?**

By sensitizing your taste buds. Here's how
you do it: Dry off your tongue as thoroughly as
possible. Now press a strip of duct tape onto your
dried tongue. Wait sixty seconds for your tongue
and the duct tape to "bond." Then yank the strip off;
your taste buds will be sensitized to bring out the
flavor in any food. It's like chemical-free
MSG on a roll. —*DTG*

What if a magic portal is opened and wild, gas-mask-wearing monkeys with chain saws for arms come in through it?

We suggest developing a healthy addiction to the ultimate power tool, duct tape, rather than the drugs you seem to have been using. —*DTG*

What if I had a javelin thrown into my forehead. How could you fix that with duct tape?

All you have to do is cover that javelin and your forehead with duct tape and get a job at the circus sideshow as the "Humanicorn." —*DTG*

I'm stranded on a desert island, and all I have is a roll of duct tape. How do I get off the island?

All you have to do is down a couple of trees, make a duct tape "hammock" between them, and raise a sail made of duct tape sheeting. There, you have a nifty-looking catamaran to sail you to safety! The shiny surface of the duct tape will also act as a beacon to signal rescue planes. —*DTG*

I wonder how they e-mailed us if they only had duct tape on a desert island?

I think it was a hypothetical question, Jim.

That's stupid, Tim! How could you get hypothermia on a desert island?

Some kids were playing baseball and hit it through our window, breaking both the window and our television screen. I can tape up the window, but how can duct tape repair my TV?

Take this opportunity to tape over the TV screen to create a new screen surface, onto which you duct tape book pages and magazine and newspaper articles for your family to *read*. You will soon come to appreciate the day when that baseball changed your viewing habits. —*DTG*

**Our lead singer left our band.
How can duct tape bring him back to us?**

The first thing you want to do is to change
your music to heavy metal. Then find a guy or gal off
the street (musical talent handy, but not required) and
encase them entirely in duct tape. Name the new
"singer" Ducttape—one word, you know, like Sting.
With all of the attention and exposure you will be
getting from your trendy new band, your old singer
will get jealous and come crawling back, begging to
be in the band once again. —*DTG*

I live in an apartment and would like to hang my pictures on the walls. Unfortunately, my landlord has informed me that I'm neither allowed to use nails in the walls nor tape on the walls. Any ideas?

The landlord didn't say that you couldn't put tape on the ceiling, right? So attach long strips of duct tape folded over onto itself to the ceiling right next to the wall wherever you want to hang your pictures. Then simply duct tape the silvery strip to the back of the pictures. Voilà! You've created an attractive duct tape gallery! —*DTG*

I broke my favorite CD into a hundred pieces. Can duct tape restore it to playable condition?

No. —*DTG*

Did our answer mean that this guy stumped us, Tim?

No. They asked if duct tape could restore the CD. We said, "No, it can't," and that is the correct answer. Therefore, they didn't stump us.

Phew! For a minute there I thought the broken CD would break our nonstumped record.

Is there any way to slice pizza with duct tape?

Make a four-by-four-foot square of duct tape on the carpeting on the far side of an open door. Next, string a few strips of duct tape tightly across the open door frame. Fling the pizza at the strips of duct tape. They should slice it nicely before it falls conveniently onto the four-by-four eating surface. —*DTG*

There is a conspiracy theory that we never actually went to the moon. Can you prove otherwise?

Heck yeah! We were there, as evidenced in these photos. —*DTG*

Can duct tape help me learn to swim?

Duct tape empty plastic milk jugs all over your upper torso—this should keep you afloat. Then just wiggle your arms and legs until you start moving. One by one, remove the milk jugs and you'll be swimming! —*DTG*

Can you use duct tape to make liquid hydrogen and liquid oxygen for rocket fuel?

Because of national security and an "agreement" that we've signed with NASA, we can't tell you the formula. However, be assured that there is duct tape involved. Oh yes! And plenty of it! —*DTG*

My pet rats chew through their water bottles. If you try to fix them with duct tape, it doesn't work. They chew through the duct tape even when I put on three layers of it. Can you give me a solution to my problem?

Stick little pellets of rat poison on the duct tape before you wrap their water bottles with it. You might lose a few in the learning curve, but it won't be too long before they figure out not to chew on duct tape. —*DTG*

We should note that we are not advocating poisoning animals, even if they are rats.

You may not be, but I am, Tim.

They're all God's creatures, Jim— how can you kill them?

Hey, I didn't kill them; the guys that make the rat poison did. They'll have to answer for their actions. I'm just trying to help this person with their water-bottle problem.

Stump THE DUCT TAPE GUYS

I have a kidney infection, and I was wondering how duct tape could possibly cure it?

We're not doctors, so this is only our best guess and not to be taken as authorized medical advice. Here's what we'd do: Take a six-inch strip of duct tape and rip it into thin threads, each about one-eighth of an inch wide. Swallow the strips, one at a time (so they don't bunch up going down your throat). As the sticky strips pass through your system, they'll probably stick to all of the infection stuff and you will eventually pass it. If that doesn't work, while you are having the emergency surgery to remove the duct tape strips, tell them to take care of your kidney infection and remove your appendix, too, while they are at it. —*DTG*

Stump the DUCT TAPE GUYS

> **I really want to get my pilet's licence,
> but I don't really have the time. How can duct
> tape help me to achieve my goal of flying?**

Who says you need a pilot's license to fly? Heck, you
can't even spell it! Duct tape yourself to the underside
of a small airplane and enjoy a free ride!
CAUTION: Spare the tape and you will find yourself
in need of a parachute. —*DTG*

It's almost Christmas here in Baltimore and we still don't have any snow. In fact, it's only just getting cold this week. Being an avid skier, I'd like to know how duct tape could be used to re-create the sensation of skiing.

Cover your eyes with white duct tape, go outside, and stare into the sun while someone pelts your face with water droplets. It will give you the illusion of being "snow-blind." As for the skiing sensation, duct tape your feet to the roof of your car and go for a forty-mile-an-hour drive down a winding road while incorporating the first two hints. —*DTG*

How can you fix a hockey stick with duct tape so it is secure? I've tried, but it is never strong enough and the broken area flops around.

You might play hockey, but you obviously don't duct tape like a hockey player! You aren't using enough duct tape, man! If you need more support than the tape affords you, use a splinting material, like a butter knife, or a coat hanger for the curved parts. If you don't trust duct tape alone to do the job, slop some wood glue into the break before you tape. Remember that duct tape comes in various "team colors," so you can customize your repair job appropriately. Tape on—and keep your stick on the ice! —*DTG*

I just had a big fight with my girlfriend and have no clue what I did to start the fight. So my question is, how can a man use duct tape to fully understand a woman?

Short of duct taping yourself to your gal twenty-four hours a day for a month or so, you may never understand what makes women tick. We suggest swallowing your pride and learning to say, "I'm sorry, honey. I was wrong. Here, let me make it up to you with this little token of my affection." After which you present her with a long-stemmed rose that you've fashioned out of duct tape. —*DTG*

Can duct tape fix my mother's ankle?

Sure! When found without their "real tools of the trade," medical professionals often resort to duct tape for splinting, suturing, etc. Will it heal completely? If you set it right and immobilize the ankle completely during the recommended healing period, sure! And when the tape is removed, Mom won't have to shave that ankle for months! —*DTG*

How can duct tape help me
make my model rockets fly straighter?

Imbalanced rockets often result in crooked flights.
Make sure your rocket is properly balanced by duct
taping small coins or paper clips onto the fuselage.
And make sure your rocket engine is sitting straight
by putting a small duct tape wedge on the errant side
of the engine chamber. We hope that helps. —DTG

> Do you think duct tape could help me drive
> straight, Tim?
>
> If you'd pay to get your wheels aligned, that
> might help, Jim.
>
> Nah, I think I'll just duct tape coins and
> paper clips on the side of my car.
>
> Huh?

How can I save money on my upcoming hernia operation by using duct tape?

Since a weakening in a muscle wall is usually the cause of a hernia, you can make an exterior muscle wall (basically a girdle) out of duct tape. This won't actually heal the weakening muscle or the hole in the muscle wall, but it will prevent you from rupturing and strangulating your hernia. So, you could probably skip the operation and live the rest of your days in a duct tape girdle. —*DTG*

I had an operation on my knee and I found out that I am allergic to topical iodine. It makes my knee itch something crazy! How can duct tape relieve the itching?

Apply duct tape on the area surrounding your incision. Then quickly rip it off. You will find that it creates a wonderful "scratching" sensation. Repeat as needed. —*DTG*

My brain itches, Tim.

Think about rubbing it with sandpaper, Jim.

Aaahhh!

On your Stump the Duct Tape Guys rules, it says to read through *all* of your archives before asking a question. I don't have that much time. How can I read all of your archives in under five minutes?

Duct tape yourself to Evelyn Wood. —*DTG*

I'm sixteen and have recently discovered that my fontanels have not been developing properly. Needless to say, I've started to worry! Is there any way that I could stimulate the development process of my fontanels with duct tape?

Your fontanels should have sealed up long ago—like by the age of two or three, for sure. If you are sixteen, they probably never will. So duct tape a metal bowl to your skull for protection. —*DTG*

Hey, Tim. Do you ever wonder why our web site gets more than its share of freaks visiting it?

Take a look in this mirror, Jim.

What? . . . oh.

How would you cure a horiblie stinkey sock with duct tape?

By duct taping over your feet before you put them into your socks. As for curing your spelling problem . . . duct tape a dictionary to your nonwriting arm. —*DTG*

I play my drums in the garage, and the neighbors are complaining. Is there any way I can soundproof the garage with duct tape?

Duct tape mattresses onto the garage walls and egg cartons onto the mattresses. Or duct tape mattresses and egg cartons to your neighbors' ears. —*DTG*

Why don't duct tape balls bounce?

Since duct tape has a rubber-based adhesive, you
would think that it would bounce better. But since it
doesn't seem to, take advantage of this and make
juggling balls out of it. They won't bounce or
roll away when you drop them. —*DTG*

Obviously, gaffers' tape is a much better product than duct tape. First of all, duct tape leaves a residue on everything. Why deal with that? Gaffers' tape never does that. Gaffers' tape is also easier to rip, and the black looks prettier than ugly gray. Eeeww, gray! I hope you take some time to consider the benefits of gaffers' tape as opposed to duct tape, and maybe next time you'll think twice before devoting an entire book to such a poor product by comparison.

Have you ever tried to fix an exhaust manifold with gaffers' tape? Or seal a heating duct? Or perform any of hundreds of thousands of other repair jobs, from plumbing to resealing disposable diapers, with gaff tape? It's just not as sticky—on purpose. Its sole job is to secure cables to the floor temporarily and to be inconspicuous while doing so. It's a first cousin of duct tape (which now comes in a huge assortment of colors—including black). So don't be so quick to write off the virtues of duct tape. We have never put down gaffers' tape! —*DTG*

Stump THE DUCT TAPE GUYS

My cat keeps climbing up the curtains and leaves rather large holes in them. Please help me.

Duct tape your curtains, sticky-side out, and your cat will lose interest quickly, since cats hate sticking to the stuff. Once the cat has lost interest, you can either remove the tape or just leave it there—eventually it will start collecting a nice layer of dust and look like fancy gray velvet curtains. —*DTG*

I play the clarinet and have recently discovered that my B-natural will not come out without squeaking. How can duct tape prevent this from happening? Also, how can duct tape make my reeds last longer? I go through a box of reeds a month!

B-natural, the thirteenth key (a sliver key), is obviously very important, since it is used in the chalumeau and clarion registers. We might suggest a number of things you can try. First, clean your pads with duct tape. Second, look for missing or leaking pads and replace them with duct tape (not sticky-side out or the tone hole will stay closed). Or your mouth may not be sporting the correct embouchure, in which case you could duct tape your mouth and jaw into the correct position so you are putting the proper pressure on the reed (tape the corners of your lips back into a smile). As for the reeds lasting longer, if you do the mouth-and-jaw taping for correct embouchure, you won't be as hard on the reeds, and they will subsequently last longer. —DTG

How could I get more channels on my satellite using only duct tape and WD-40?

You could cut your neighbor's cable, splice in the line going from your satellite dish to your television, cover the splice with duct tape, and bury the cable. Presto! More channels! Or get a bunch of aluminum pie plates and duct tape them all over the circumference of your dish—this will broaden the pickup area, extend the focus range of the dish, and bring in more channels (we think). *—DTG*

Where does duct tape rank in the diet of mice?

Fortunately, mice don't eat duct tape. If they did, they'd have a field day in our houses. *—DTG*

Stump THE DUCT TAPE GUYS

I'm a concert pianist, and I have a performance in two days. The middle E string broke, though it is very unusual to break a string. I tried duct taping right on the string to connect them together, but the note won't play when something stops the vibration of the string. What should I do?

You can either play around that note or duct tape an E tuning fork in the spot vacated by the broken string. —*DTG*

Stump the Duct Tape Guys

I am a redneck and I want to know
how I can turn my riding mower into an
excavator using only duct tape?

Take off the mower deck and duct tape it to
the front of your rider. Plow on, dude!
By the way, you're not fooling us for a second.
Real rednecks don't have e-mail! —*DTG*

Stump THE DUCT TAPE GUYS

How is it possible to live life without duct tape?

That's not a real question!
You KNOW it's not possible.
Jeez, don't waste our time! —*DTG*

Hey, Tim, what do you think we'd do
if duct tape didn't exist?

I don't know about you, but since we've
gotten all the free duct tape we want
just because we wrote books about
duct tape, I'd probably try to be
"Hundred-Dollar Bill Guy."

Good thinking, Tim.

Thanks, Jim.

**Why does tape stick? What properties
of duct tape adhesive makes it stick so well?**

We're not chemists or physicists, but our guess is that
the rubber-based adhesive coupled with the
polyethylene backing provide the flex that allows for
good adhesion, while the fabric in the center gives it
strength. If you need more technical information
than that, we suggest that you contact
a duct tape manufacturer. —*DTG*

I want to duct tape a guy's car—the whole thing. I want to know, though, if duct tape would remove the paint from his car.

You would not be well advised to duct tape someone's car without their permission—or unless it has an absolutely hideous paint job to start with. The duct tape probably won't remove the paint, but it *will* leave a residue. —*DTG*

Yeah, live and learn, right, Jim?

How many times do I have to apologize, Tim?

I still have leaves from last fall sticking to my car!

This girl said, "If duct tape can do everything, then why don't I use it to clear up your acne?" So is this possible without putting it on my face?

Ouch! Some chicks just have no tact! Well, since some acne is caused by what you eat, put it over your mouth to avoid the ingestion of the wrong foods. No, wait. You didn't want to put it on your face. . . . Okay, duct tape your wrists to your hips and your hands will not be able to lift food to your mouth. Some acne is caused by stress. You can destress by lying on the couch with your eyes closed and reciting this mantra: "Duct tape, duct tape, duct tape . . ." Repeat until your stress has melted away and, soon, so will your zits. Until they do, duct tape over that girl's eyes so she won't be so bothered so much by your acne. —*DTG*

How can duct tape make a bake sale more profitable?

Jim and I are suckers for a good pie! Tell us where your bake sale is and we'll be the honorary judges of the pie-tasting contest. Our presence should bring in hordes of duct tape lovers (along with their dollars). Or just skip the baked goods and sell rolls of duct tape. —*DTG*

My ears hurt a lot when my nose is stuffy. Is there a way that duct tape can be used to unplug my nose and stop the ear pain?

Duct tape two of those tubes of menthol smelly stuff right up each nostril and it'll probably help your nose clear out. Until then, duct tape a folded sock over each ear to keep them warm and cozy. —*DTG*

I read somewhere that you can make a Christmas wreath out of red and green duct tape. I can't find the article. Can you help me?

While we don't know the exact duct tape Christmas wreath directions you're referring to, we would simply wrap green duct tape around an old tire and add a big red duct tape bow. However, if you are a Martha Stewart wannabe (i.e., have *way* too much time on your hands), rip four hundred twelve-inch strips of green duct tape, fold them over onto themselves, and cut fringes in each side of the six-inch strips. Duct tape the four hundred fringed green duct tape strips around a hula hoop, add a big red duct tape bow, and presto—you have a charming Christmas wreath that will never drop its needles and will surely gather lots of positive comments from your holiday guests for years to come. Duct tape: It's like Martha Stewart on a roll . . . only a lot less irritating! —*DTG*

My brother and dad won't stop playing with baseball cards. They stare at them night and day! How can I get them to notice me?

We were going to suggest duct taping cards to yourself, but that's too obvious—you've probably already thought of that. Start collecting duct tape books (this is book seven in our collection). Then start making stuff out of duct tape: flowers, wallets, clothing, car accessories, etc. Soon they'll see that you are having a lot more fun than they are and will join you in your creative endeavors. Remember, the family that duct tapes together sticks together. —*DTG*

How can I get my dog to lose weight without duct taping his mouth closed?

Duct tape Fido on an outrigger taped to the side of your bicycle and go for a five-mile ride. Do this every day for a month and your dog will lose weight. —*DTG*

How can you sharpen a pencil with duct tape?

Duct tape the pencil at an angle to the side of your shoe—eraser end facing forward. Drag that foot when you walk and the lead end of the pencil will wear off into a nice sharp point. —*DTG*

Jim, maybe we could duct tape you to my shoe to sharpen your wit!

Very funny, Tim.

You know how gross canned peas are, right?
Well, how can you fix the taste of a
can of peas with duct tape?

We thought they were supposed to taste that way. In
fact, Tim likes 'em! If you don't like the taste of
something, you might try duct taping over your
tongue. That way, stuff can pass over your taste buds
without leaving any flavor behind. —*DTG*

I have curly hair, and I want straight hair! How can duct tape help me achieve my goal?

Duct tape lead fishing sinkers to the ends of your hair and it will straighten out in no time! —*DTG*

How can I achieve world domination using only duct tape?

We aren't permitted to tell you. —*DTG*

I live just outside of the city of Philadelphia, Pennsylvania. The freeways into the city are often jammed. How can duct tape solve this?

We were just in Philly and didn't find the traffic to be all that bad. Of course, it could have been because we took the wrong exit to the airport and ended up driving through the projects. But we did find people to be filled with the brotherly love that your town is noted for. Here's what you do: Grab a roll of black and a roll of white duct tape. Go out at three in the morning and change the directional signs on the freeway to route commuters onto the exits and out of your way. The next day you can enjoy a jam-free commute (or room and board provided at the city's expense). —*DTG*

When our sun starts to die, it will first become much larger. That means it will engulf the first four planets and burn everything on them to a nice fiery black. How can we use duct tape to prevent this but still have light so that we don't freeze to death?

This will not happen in our lifetime, so don't worry about it. Go duct tape something. —*DTG*

How can you stop a duct tape lover from loving duct tape using only duct tape?

Wow! Certainly not by taking it away—absence
only makes the heart grow fonder. Certainly not
by giving them more duct tape—there can never
be too much duct tape. Until they come out with
a product more versatile than duct tape . . .

I guess you've *stumped us!*

Dang, Tim. We almost made it all the way through the book without being stumped!

Yeah, I hate for it to end that way, Jim, but we've run out of pages.

Let's just leave that last one out of the book.

Too late, Jim. It's already printed. Let's go duct tape something.

Okay.

Got a pressing question
that hasn't been
answered here? Visit
www.DuctTapeGuys.com
and click on
"Stump the Duct Tape Guys."

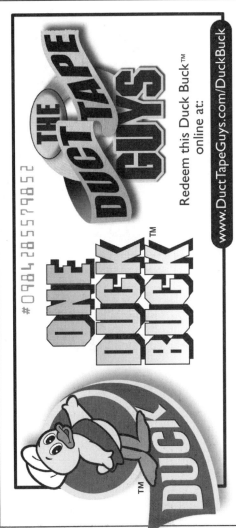

YOU GOT THE BOOK NOW GET FREE STUFF!

TURN THIS PAGE OVER TO REDEEM YOUR DUCK BUCK NOW!

Make sure you complete this information:

name

address

city

state _____ zip

email